Bella
Loves Bugs

happy yak

Text © 2022 Jess French
Illustration © 2022 Duncan Beedie

Jess French has asserted her right to be identified as the author of this work. Duncan Beedie has asserted his right to be identified as the illustrator of this work.

Designer: Mike Henson
Commissioning Editor: Carly Madden
Editor: Victoria Garrard
Creative Director: Malena Stojić
Associate Publisher: Rhiannon Findlay

First published in 2022 by Happy Yak, an imprint of The Quarto Group.
100 Cummings Center, Suite 265D Beverly, MA 01915, USA.
T (978) 282-9590 F (978) 283-2742
www.quarto.com

A CIP record for this book is available from the Library of Congress.

ISBN 978 0 7112 6562 2

Manufactured in Guangdong, China TT012022

9 8 7 6 5 4 3 2 1

MIX
Paper from responsible sources
FSC® C016973

STAY SAFE!

Bug hunting is great fun if you follow these guidelines:

- Take a grown-up with you to keep you safe.

- Always treat bugs kindly and only touch them if a grown-up tells you it's ok.

- Always wash your hands with soap and water after touching bugs.

- If you are unsure what a bug is, don't touch it!

- Never touch the wings of bugs.

- Always put bugs back where you found them.

JESS FRENCH

DUNCAN BEEDIE

Bella Loves Bugs

I'm Nancy, a house spider. I'm never far away from Bella so keep an eye out for me!

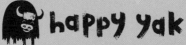
happy yak

HELLO, I'M BELLA. I LOVE BUGS.
When I grow up, I want to be an
entomologist—that's someone
who studies insects.

My dad is helping me
collect garlic mustard
to feed to my hungry
caterpillars.

Caterpillars can be very fussy—
some of them will only eat the
leaves of one or two specific plants.

Sometimes I bring insects inside so I can learn
more about them, but I always put them back
out in the wild when I have finished.

Caterpillars should be
kept in a container with
air holes and fresh food,
away from direct sunlight.

Here you go, caterpillars. Some fresh leaves to help you grow big and strong.

Oh! I prefer fly soup.

Caterpillars have just one job and that is to eat! They grow bigger and bigger until they have enough energy to make a special case called a chrysalis.

Time to go exploring! I'll just grab my things...

One of my caterpillars has already made its chrysalis. Inside it's busy turning into a butterfly. I can't wait to see what it looks like!

Once you start bug hunting, you'll realize that bugs are everywhere!

You don't need any special equipment to find them, but there are a few things that can help...

SCRAPBOOK OR NOTEBOOK— to record the things you see.

COLLECTING JAR —to get a closer look at the bugs.

SWEEP NET —to catch insects in long grass.

POND-DIPPING KIT —to look for bugs underwater.

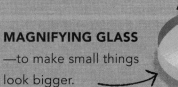

MAGNIFYING GLASS —to make small things look bigger.

ID GUIDE —to identify bugs. It's important that you don't get too close to bugs unless you have identified them and know that it's safe.

Wearing the right clothes is important too. Bugs come out in all weathers. Entomologists must be prepared for SUN...

... or RAIN!

Wheeee!

Ok, I'm all packed. Time to go!

"Hi Bella, I've just been looking at some birds through my binoculars, which make things that are far away look bigger."

"Hi Billy. You're always looking at birds! My magnifying glass makes things look bigger too. Would you like to see?"

"Look! It's a line of ants. They're carrying food."

Ants are very strong, they can lift things that weigh many times their own body weight.

Ants are insects, which means they have six legs and a body split up into three parts. Let's take a closer look...

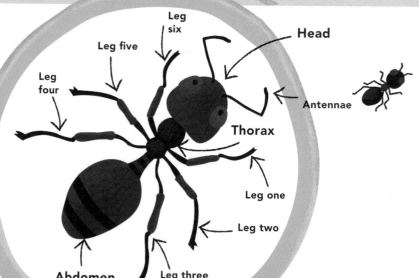

Leg six

Leg five

Leg four

Head

Antennae

Thorax

Leg one

Leg two

Leg three

Abdomen

AWESOME ANTS

Ants live all over the world.
Some of them have special superpowers.

Saharan silver ants are the speediest of all the ants, they race across the desert so they don't spend too long in the sun.

Bullet ants have a nasty bite.

Leafcutter ants use cut-up bits of leaf to grow fungus, which they eat.

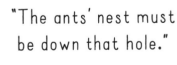

I prefer to let my food come to me.

"The ants' nest must be down that hole."

Inside an ants' nest

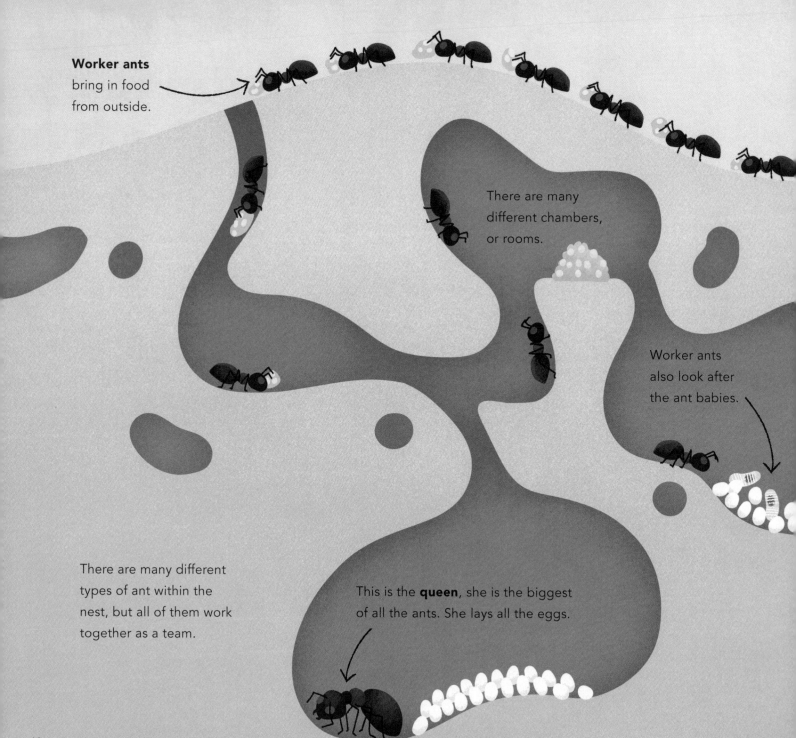

Worker ants bring in food from outside.

There are many different chambers, or rooms.

Worker ants also look after the ant babies.

There are many different types of ant within the nest, but all of them work together as a team.

This is the **queen**, she is the biggest of all the ants. She lays all the eggs.

"Ants are so good at looking out for one another."

"Yes, they are! Other insects work together as a team too."

Where's my team?

SOCIAL INSECTS

Insects that live and work together in big groups are called social insects.

Termites

Bees

Paper wasps

Ants

Hornets

"There's a bee!"

"It's buzzing around the flowers, searching for a sweet juice called nectar!"

BUZZZZ!

TYPES OF BEE

Bumblebee

Leaf-cutter bee

Mining bee

Mason bee

Wool carder bee

Honeybee

Carpenter bee

"It's a **honeybee** so it will share the nectar it collects with the other members of its hive."

"Maybe it's going back to the beehive! Let's go!"

The buzzing sound that bees make comes from the movement of their wings.

BUZZZZ!

Bees feed on the sugary nectar found inside flowers.

Flying uses up lots of energy, so bees need to eat a lot of nectar.

I'm looking for the buzz stop!

"Can you see the yellow balls on the bee's legs? That's pollen!"

Bees help fruit and vegetables grow by carrying pollen from flower to flower. This is called pollination.

"It's important that we protect bees. Without them lots of plants and flowers would disappear."

CHIRRUP!

"That wasn't a bee!"

It wasn't me!

Can you guess what is making that noise?

"It's a grasshopper! I will try and catch it with my sweep net."

SWOOSH!

SWOOSH!

SWOOSH!

The grasshopper is very hard to catch! It leaps about using its powerful legs.

"Grasshoppers are such good jumpers! Imagine if we could jump as far as them!"

HOP!

HOP!

HOP!

Other bugs are great jumpers too. Let's take a look...

Can you hop like a grasshopper?

17

Bouncing bugs

Fleas leap from animal to animal, sucking their blood.

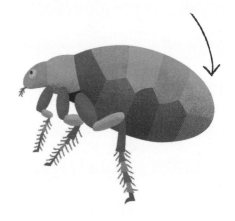

Crickets look a lot like grasshoppers but have longer antennae, or feelers, and flatter bodies.

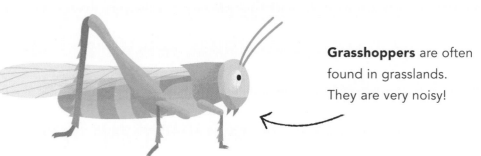

Grasshoppers are often found in grasslands. They are very noisy!

Froghoppers are the most impressive of all the jumping insects. They can jump 100 times their own length!

Click beetles use a snapping movement to fling themselves into the air, which makes a loud "click" sound.

"I've caught something but it's not a grasshopper...

...it's a butterfly!"

"I will let it go carefully so that I don't damage its wings. Look how it flutters."

"Where are you off to, fluttery butterfly?"

19

The butterfly flies from flower to flower in search of nectar, just like the bee.

It's so colorful! It's hard to believe that one of my wriggly caterpillars will turn into a beautiful butterfly like this.

A butterfly has a long tongue, which it uses to slurp up nectar.

This is a **monarch butterfly**. It has brightly colored wings to warn other animals that it's poisonous to eat.

Many bugs that are red, orange, or yellow are poisonous.

Butterflies soak up heat from the sun to give them energy.

BEAUTIFUL BUTTERFLIES

Butterflies come in lots of different shapes and colors.

Glasswing butterflies have wings that are see-through.

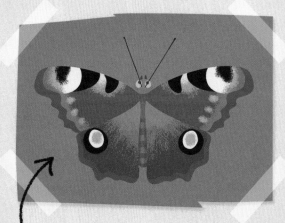

Peacock butterflies have spots on their wings that look like eyes.

Blue morpho butterflies shimmer in the sunlight.

Birdwing butterflies have huge and brightly colored wings.

Orange oakleaf butterflies have wings that look like leaves.

The butterfly is laying some eggs!

Monarch butterflies lay their eggs on milkweed plants.

Butterfly lifecycle

As well as growing bigger as they grow older, butterflies change shape too! This is called their lifecycle.

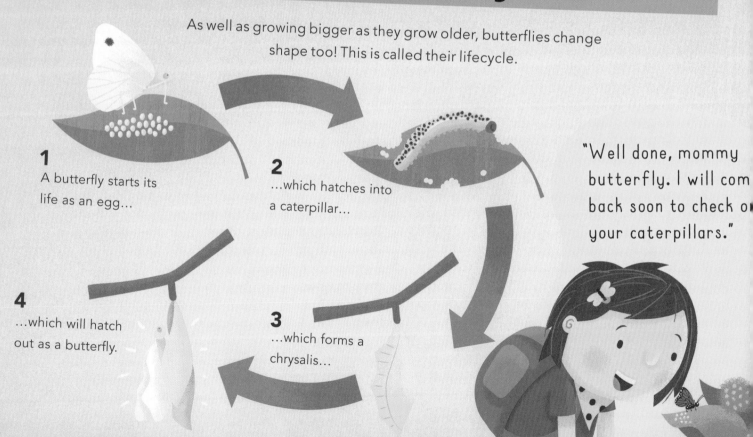

1
A butterfly starts its life as an egg...

2
...which hatches into a caterpillar...

3
...which forms a chrysalis...

4
...which will hatch out as a butterfly.

"Well done, mommy butterfly. I will com
back soon to check o
your caterpillars."

The air is full of flying insects today!
A dragonfly just zoomed past.

It's heading toward the pond. There are
always lots of insects down there...

I can fly
tooooo!

ZOOOOOOM!

Wow, look at that group of **pond skaters** zipping around the surface of the water. They are so fast!

Always go pond dipping with an adult and make sure to find a safe place to kneel beside the pond, not too close to the edge.

There are lots of amazing bugs hiding below the surface of the water too. I'm going to do some pond dipping to see what I can find.

This white tray will help us to see the things we have found more clearly.

First, fill your tray with pond water.

I must be careful not to stir up the mud at the bottom of the pond.

SCOOP...

SCOOP...

You could make your own net from a wire hanger and an old pair of tights.

Sweep your net slowly through the water, then tip the contents gently out into the tray.

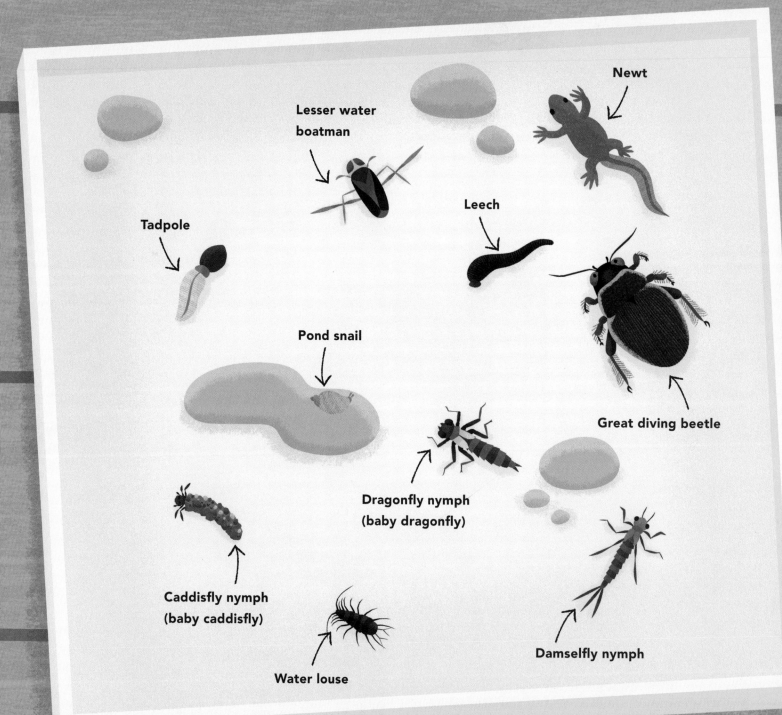

Newt

Lesser water
boatman

Leech

Tadpole

Great diving beetle

Pond snail

Dragonfly nymph
(baby dragonfly)

Caddisfly nymph
(baby caddisfly)

Damselfly nymph

Water louse

Let's take a closer look at the baby dragonfly.

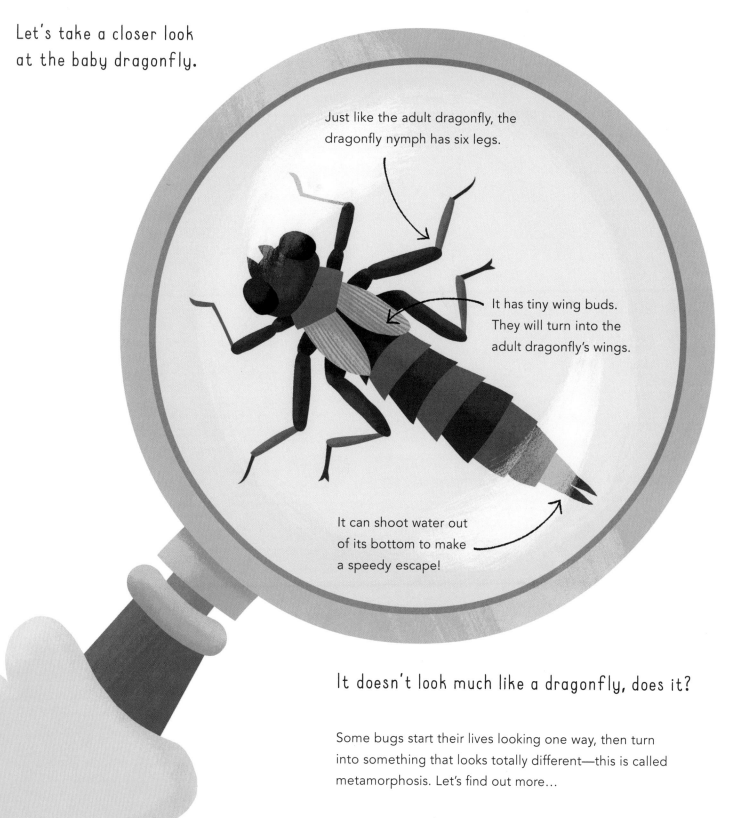

Just like the adult dragonfly, the dragonfly nymph has six legs.

It has tiny wing buds. They will turn into the adult dragonfly's wings.

It can shoot water out of its bottom to make a speedy escape!

It doesn't look much like a dragonfly, does it?

Some bugs start their lives looking one way, then turn into something that looks totally different—this is called metamorphosis. Let's find out more...

Marvelous metamorphosis

Many bugs completely change their body shape over the course of their lives.

1. Most bugs start as eggs.

2. Then they turn into a larva. This stage is all about eating! The larva must grow big and strong so that it has enough energy to metamorphose (change shape).

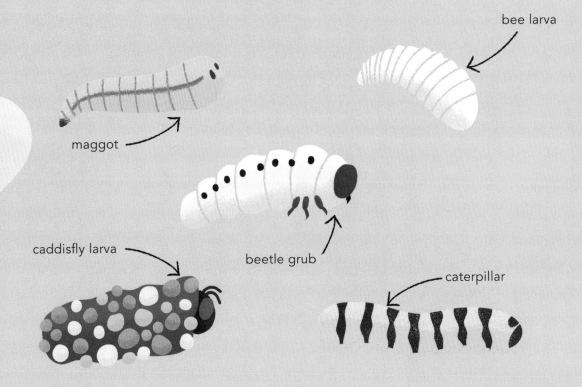

bee larva

maggot

caddisfly larva

beetle grub

caterpillar

3. When it has grown enough, it makes a case called a pupa.
At this stage, the animal can look much the same from the outside, but
inside it is rearranging its body parts to become something totally new!

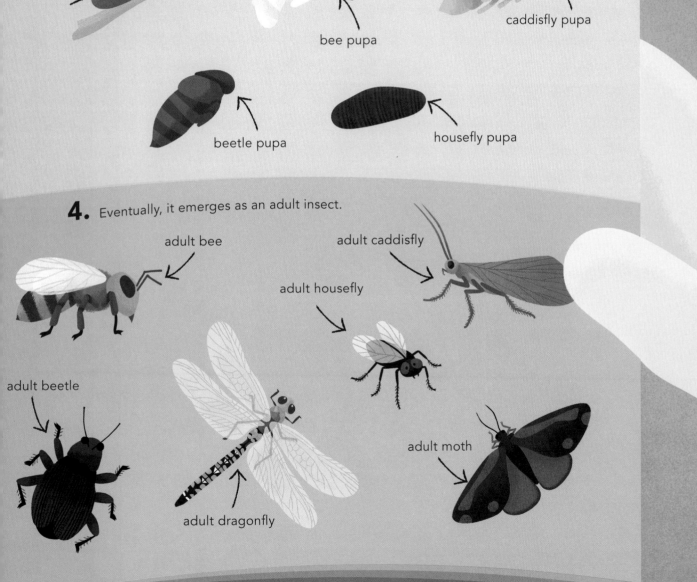

moth pupa

bee pupa

caddisfly pupa

beetle pupa

housefly pupa

4. Eventually, it emerges as an adult insect.

adult bee

adult caddisfly

adult housefly

adult beetle

adult dragonfly

adult moth

The caddisfly larva is funny-looking, isn't it?
It makes a case for itself by spinning together
any materials it can find with silk.

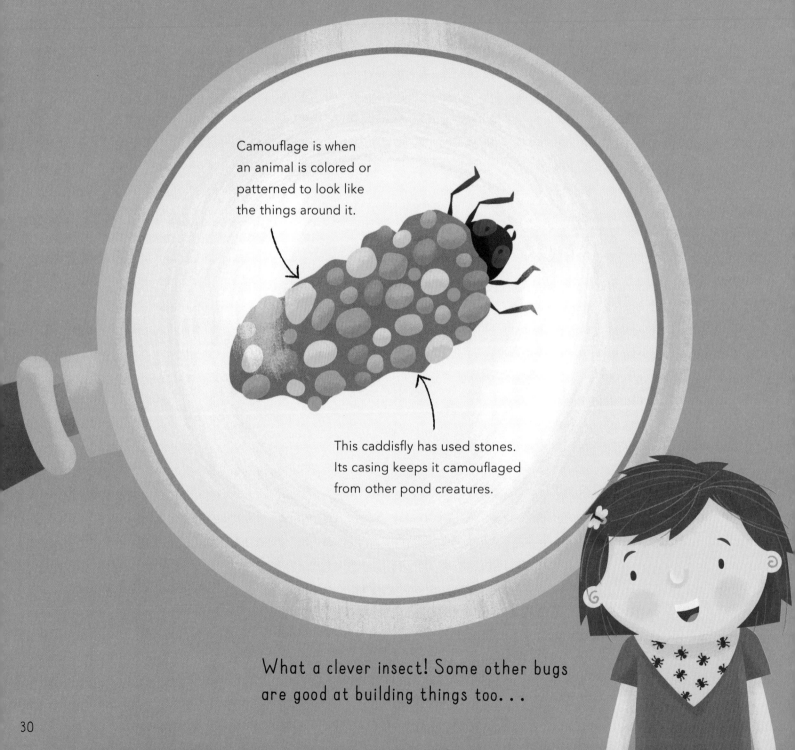

Camouflage is when
an animal is colored or
patterned to look like
the things around it.

This caddisfly has used stones.
Its casing keeps it camouflaged
from other pond creatures.

What a clever insect! Some other bugs
are good at building things too...

Built by bugs

Wasp nest
It's hard to believe that these beautiful structures are made of chewed-up wood mixed with wasp saliva!

Spider web
Made of super-strong spider silk, sticky spider webs trap food for the spider to eat.

Termite mound
Probably the most incredible of all the structures built by insects, termite mounds can be as tall as a grown-up.

That reminds me, I built a trap in the woods yesterday. Time to go and see what I've caught. Bye, pond bugs! Back in the water you go.

31

My trap is hidden under a rock by this path. I love the forest, every rock and stone provides a bug habitat.

A habitat is a place that provides the right conditions for an animal to live in.

I wonder what's under this one...

...a family of woodlice!

Woodlice are crustaceans, more closely related to crabs and lobsters than insects.

They've got more legs than me!

Impressive!

Some of the woodlice have curled up into balls because they are scared. I will put the rock back to make them feel safer.

I wonder what's under here...

A wolf spider and her eggs!

Wolf spiders are very caring mothers. When her babies hatch they will ride around on her back.

I have placed a yogurt cup under this rock. It acts as a tumble trap. When a bug tumbles in, it can't get out again because of its slippy sides. I wonder if I have caught anything...

To build a tumble trap, dig a hole in the ground with a trowel. Pop a yogurt cup in the hole then cover it with a stone or a tile. Prop it up with stones or twigs. Now, go away and wait...

I can hear something scuttling inside. How exciting!

Putting cheese or fruit inside your trap can help to tempt minibeasts inside.

Oh wow! It's a stag beetle! It has huge jaws, which it uses to fight other stag beetles.

Don't be upset, stag beetle, I will set you free.

It is very important to set free any insects that you trap.

Plastic is very bad for the environment so I will take this cup with me.

Oh, but what's underneath it?

Stag beetle grub

Worm

Amazing! This grub will turn into a stag beetle, like the one I found in my tumble trap.

It has strong jaws, which it uses to chomp through wood.

Twelve brilliant beetles

Ladybug
Brightly colored
to warn other
animals that they
taste nasty.

Goliath beetle
Heaviest of all
the beetles.

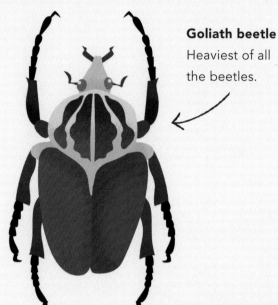

Giraffe-necked weevil
One of the weirdest-
looking insects.

Rhinoceros beetle
Like stag beetles, they have
huge horns for fighting.

Dung beetles
Collect animal poop.

Cockchafer beetle
Very noisy fliers.

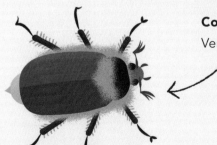

Rainbow leaf beetle
Have rainbow-patterned
wing cases.

Wasp beetle
Looks like a wasp to
scare off predators.

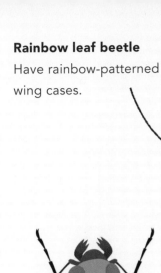

Green tiger beetle
A super-speedy runner.

Whirligig beetle
Swims in circles
underwater.

Bombardier beetle
Sprays hot acid from its bottom.

Burying beetles
Gets rid of dead animals
by burying them.

Yay, it's started raining. That means all sorts of interesting creatures will come out to play!

"Hi, Ava! What have you got there?"

"This is my wormery! I'm looking for **worms** to put inside."

"That looks great. I bet the worms love tunneling through all that soil. I'm looking for bugs that come out in the rain too."

A wormery is a container where worms turn waste food and kitchen scraps into compost.

Ah ha, a slimy trail. That's sure to lead to some slimy minibeasts...

Hey, what are you doing up there?

WOW!

Slime is so sticky that **snails** can even hold on when they're upside down!

Slugs and **snails** love the rain!

Slugs and snails must always stay wet. They need water to make their sticky slime.

Sorry slug, I didn't mean to scare you!

If slugs are scared, they can blow bubbles in their slime.

I will put the slug back to finish its leafy dinner. It will be getting dark soon, so I should head home.

Before I go inside, I will check on the
minibeasts living in my bug hotel, which
I made with all kinds of pots and twigs.
Let's see who's under the flowerpots.

Three-night
mini-break,
here I come!

Ohh, today's hotel visitors have lots of legs!

Centipedes are very speedy scuttlers. Look at all its legs!

Centipedes have wide, flat bodies, so they can squeeze into tight spaces—like underneath flowerpots.

Centipede

A millipede has even more legs than the centipede!

Millipede

Millipedes have long, rounded bodies, perfect for burying down into the soil. Millipedes are slow and steady, trundling along on their many small legs.

Its legs are right underneath its body. They look a bit like the bristles of a toothbrush.

It's nearly bedtime for me, but for some bugs, it's time to wake up!

I'm going to have a quick sneak peek at some of these nighttime insects before I go to sleep.

Wow, look at those bright, flashing lights. They are fireflies, flashing to attract a mate.

So beautiful!

Some insects make their own light, but others are attracted to our light. Maybe I can attract some more bugs to the balcony by shining a torch.

Moths have fluttery wings, feathery feelers and often come out at night.

You can attract moths by hanging up a white sheet and shining a light on or through it.

Just like butterflies, moths start their lives as caterpillars. I wonder what my caterpillars have been up to today...

At night I turn into a *spy*-der!

43

They look even bigger than they did this morning!
They've been gobbling up lots of leaves.

MUNCH, MUNCH!

Two more caterpillars have made their chrysalises.

Ohh, what's happening?

TWITCH   TWITCH

The butterfly is hatching out!

The butterfly's wings will dry overnight and tomorrow it can be released. Then maybe it will be able to mate and lay some eggs of its own.

Wow, you've changed...

Butterfly wings are covered in thousands of tiny scales. They are very delicate so you must never touch them.

Time for bed now, but bugs are everywhere, even inside our houses.

This housefly must have been attracted by the light and got trapped inside.

BUZZZ.

That fly was lucky not to get eaten by Nancy, our **house spider**. I wonder where she's got to. She makes the most fantastic webs.

I leave this towel hanging over the edge of the bath so that if Nancy falls in she won't get trapped by its slippy sides.

Ah, there you are! Goodnight, Nancy.
Hope you've had a good day.

It's tiring being an entomologist!
But what a great day of bug
hunting. I can't wait to release
the butterflies tomorrow.

Many spiders build a
new web every day.
Sometimes they recycle
the old silk by eating it!

Tomorrow is
web-building day!

No matter how many amazing
bugs you find, there are always
more to see. What will you
find tomorrow? Night, night!

47

HOW TO BE A
NATURE HERO
≥ BUGS ≤

Bugs are great, aren't they? They play such a big part in keeping the world functioning as it should. It's our duty as humans to protect bugs, and make the world a happier and safer place for them to live. Try the tips below to become a real life BUG HERO!

- Never use chemicals that kill bugs, such as pesticides and slug pellets.

- Build your own bug hotel and see which creatures move in!

- Grow plants such as buddleia, ivy, and cornflowers to provide nectar for bugs all year round.

- If you have a garden, leave some of the grass to grow long. Many bugs love to hide in it.

- Turn off your outside lights at night, so you don't confuse moths and other nocturnal bugs.

To protect all animals and the world they live in, it is also important to:

- Think carefully before buying new things. Try to avoid buying plastic and buy things second-hand whenever you can.

- Treat wild spaces with kindness – pick up litter, stick to the paths, and never trample on plants or fungi.

- Grow green things wherever you can. Pack your windowsill with plants or create a vegetable patch.

Pedro   Ava   Billy